Timeline

1500

European explorers discover parts of Africa and India... it is the beginning of the Age of Discovery.

1728

James Cook is born on 7th November in Yorkshire, to a large farming family.

1660

England establishes its Royal Navy, used for warfare and exploration.

1522

Ferdinand Magellan, a Portuguese explorer, finishes sailing all the way around the world. This is the first 'circumnavigation' of the globe.

1755

Aged sixteen, Cook joins the Royal Navy.

1764

After many scientific and technological advancements, the HMS Dolphin embarks upon the Royal Navy's first scientific voyage.

1772-1775

Cook's second voyage. He sails to the Antarctic and discovers many more islands in the Pacific Ocean.

1779

Arguments break out between the native Hawaiians and Captain Cook's crew. Cook is killed by a Hawaiian chief on 14th February.

1776

Captain Cook's third and final voyage for the Royal Navy. He tries to find the Northwest Passage to explore new lands, but instead finds Hawaii.

1768-1771

The now-Captain Cook sets sail on his first three-year voyage. He discovers new islands and charts parts of New Zealand.

Captain Cook's first journey to Australia

Captain Cook and the crew of his ship HMS Endeavour first landed on the continent at what is now known as Botany Bay on the Kurnell Peninsula in Sydney, New South Wales.

They then moved northwards along the coastline to Bustard Head in modern-day Queensland. The crew of the Endeavour continued past the northernmost point of Cape York Peninsula, then through the Torres Strait between Australia and Papa New Guinea until they landed at Possession Island off the coast of northern Queensland.

After this, the Endeavour left Australia behind, heading towards Savu, an island in Indonesia.

Author:
Mark Bergin studied at Eastbourne College of Art and has specialised in historical reconstructions, aviation and maritime subjects for over twenty years. He lives in Bexhill-on-Sea with his wife and three children.

Artist:
David Antram was born in Brighton, England, in 1958. He studied at Eastbourne College of Art and then worked in advertising for fifteen years before becoming a full-time artist. He has illustrated many children's non-fiction books.

Series Creator:
David Salariya was born in Dundee, Scotland. He has illustrated a wide range of books and has created and designed many new series for publishers both in the UK and overseas. In 1989, he established The Salariya Book Company. He lives in Brighton with his wife, illustrator Shirley Willis, and their son Jonathan.

Editors: **Jenny Vaughn, Sophie Izod**

Consultant: **John Woolley**
Captain Cook Memorial Museum, Whitby

Published in Great Britain in MMXVIII by Book House, an imprint of
The Salariya Book Company Ltd
25 Marlborough Place, Brighton BN1 1UB
www.salariya.com

ISBN: 978-1-912233-47-2

SALARIYA
SCRIBO BOOK HOUSE SCRIBBLERS

1 3 5 7 9 8 6 4 2

A CIP catalogue record for this book is available from the British Library.
Printed and bound in China.

Visit
www.salariya.com
for our online catalogue and
free fun stuff.

PAPER FROM
SUSTAINABLE
FORESTS

You Wouldn't Want to Explore With™

Captain Cook!

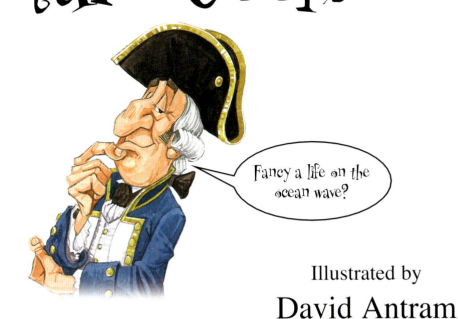

Fancy a life on the ocean wave?

Written by
Mark Bergin

Illustrated by
David Antram

Created and designed by
David Salariya

A Voyage You'd Rather Not Make

BOOK HOUSE
a SALARIYA imprint

Contents

Introduction

It's the year 1768. King George III is on the throne and Britain is expanding its horizons and finding new territories. You are sixteen-year-old Isaac Smith, and you hope to find adventure and excitement when you join the Royal Navy. James Cook, a relative of yours, is a well-respected ship's commander. Your parents have persuaded him to let you sail with him, and you're all ready to go. There's an expedition to Tahiti, all set to leave harbour. What will you see on the way? What will it be like when you get there? You have heard strange stories of people, lands and animals on the other side of the world. Will the people be friendly, or are they bloodthirsty cannibals? You think it's going to be fun – but how much do you really know about becoming a sailor? Are you sure you want to sail to the other side of the world? The voyage will take three long years – but you don't know this yet. You will have to learn the ropes and get used to your new shipmates. Your life on board an eighteenth-century square-rigged ship will be hard and dangerous. You'll have to behave yourself, or you'll be whipped! You may learn that you wouldn't want to sail with Captain Cook!

Pressed into service!

You're lucky that your parents know Captain Cook. They have asked him to take you as midshipman (officer in training) on his next voyage. For other sailors, things aren't so easy. Normally, Press Gangs recruit men to serve in the lower ranks of the Royal Navy. Squads of sailors go to public houses to round up men aged 16 to 35. Drunks are often bundled away for a life at sea before they know what's happening. Troublesome characters are knocked on the head – and wake up on board ship! Judges often give criminals and smugglers who appear in their courts a choice: join the Navy or go to prison!

ISAAC SMITH, age 16

LUCKY BREAK. Captain James Cook will take you on board his ship.

Hmm...have you ever been to sea before, young man?

Cook's mission

Captain Cook's mission is to observe the transit of Venus across the face of the Sun above the skies of Tahiti. There was a transit in 1761. Astronomers took over 120 measurements from all over the world, but their results were too different to be useful. The next transit will be on 3rd June, 1769 – and then not again for another 105 years! The mission is urgent. After the first task is done, Captain Cook also has some secret orders. For many years there has been talk of a great southern continent, called Terra Australis Incognita. Cook will look for and then chart this land.

The Route of The Endeavour:

The *Endeavour* sailed to Tahiti via South America.

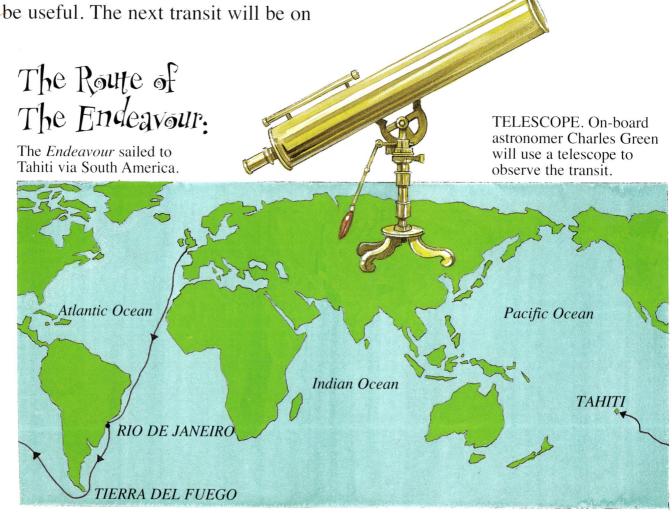

TELESCOPE. On-board astronomer Charles Green will use a telescope to observe the transit.

Atlantic Ocean

Pacific Ocean

Indian Ocean

TAHITI

RIO DE JANEIRO

TIERRA DEL FUEGO

Cast off!

Your ship is an ex-Whitby collier (coal-carrier), the *Earl of Pembroke*, bought by the Navy for £2,800 and renamed the Endeavour. It has been refitted with extra cabins for the officers and scientists. Captain Cook likes colliers because they have a shallow draught (this means they don't sit too deeply in the water). The *Endeavour* is described as 'fit to stow provisions and stores'. It is 32 m long, 10 m across at its widest, and about 4 m deep.

MEET YOUR MATES. Make friends with your shipmates, however frightening they look! Remember, you'll be spending the next three years with them.

We'll show you the ropes.

Handy hint

Get to know nautical names for parts of the ship. You'll need to know what everyone's talking about!

THE *ENDEAVOUR*. There are three masts: the fore, main and mizzen. The main is about 40 m high. These masts are supported by ropes called stays and shrouds. Ratlines, fixed to the shrouds, form ladders.

Keeping a tight ship

Discipline and punishment on board ship is hard. Punishment is often flogging – being whipped with a special whip called a 'cat-o-nine-tails'. The phrase 'over a barrel' means being tied over a gun barrel to be flogged. Captain Cook knows that if he doesn't give enough lashes, the crew won't respect him, but if he gives too many, they might mutiny! On 16th September, 1768, Henry Stephens gets twelve lashes for refusing to eat his allowance of fresh beef – sailors are used to salted meat. But Captain Cook is a reasonable man for his time and, in the three years of the voyage, he only punishes 21 men. The normal number of lashes is 12, though two men who desert get 24.

Good Discipline

Good discipline means that the ship is well ordered. Men are punished if they fail to do their duty and put the ship and crew in danger. Some of the worst offences are falling asleep on duty, refusing to follow orders, or 'unclean behaviour.'

They rub salt into the wounds too.

Jobs on Board The Endeavour:

SAIL-MAKER. He is a vital member of the crew. He mends torn and worn sails, and sometimes makes new ones.

PAINTING. Paint protects the wood and makes a good impression in port. It also keeps the crew out of trouble!

CAULKING. These men hammer greased hemp rope fibers into the plank seams of the decks, to keep the water out.

'SWAB THE DECKS!' This means cleaning the decks. It is done every morning by swabbers.

Watch out – officers!

Armourer

Gunner

Surgeon

Cook

Marine Sergeant

Lieutenant (second-in-command)

Captain Cook

ook is called 'Captain' as a courtesy. He is in charge of the *Endeavour*, with other officers supporting him. He has enormous powers. Other captains rule by the lash and are feared by all their crews. But Cook is respected for his even-handed approach to running the ship. But conditions are still hard and unpleasant.

WHO'S WHO? As well as officers, there are warrant officers and petty officers. Warrant officers: The Master navigates. The Marine Sergeant commands the ten Marines on board. The Surgeon treats illness and wounds. Petty officers: The Armourer looks after the muskets and cutlasses. The Gunner looks after the cannons, ammunition, and gunpowder. The Carpenter makes spare parts for the ship. The Boatswain (or Bosun) is in charge of the stores and setting the crew to work. The Quartermaster steers. The Cook… cooks.

Disagreements and fights sometimes break out, and it is up to the officers on board and, finally, the Captain to make sure the ship runs smoothly and everything is ship-shape! As a midshipman, if you want to become a full officer, you will need to take your lieutenant's examination in six years.

Handy hint

Follow your orders well and quickly, and you'll get along fine with Captain Cook!

Joseph Banks (Botanist)

Quartermaster

THE SCIENTIFIC TEAM. Its leader is Joseph Banks, a member of the Royal Society. Banks is wealthy and young. He's a respected, self-taught natural scientist. Daniel Solander, a Swedish naturalist, is Banks's librarian. Sydney Parkinson, a Scottish artist, will record the exotic places and plants they find.

Sydney Parkinson (Artist)

Daniel Solander (Naturalist)

Accidents will happen....

Watch out while you are on board ship! Accidents can happen anytime on long sea voyages on a square-rigger. The ship is complicated to sail, and there's always the danger that a sailor can fall from the rigging or overboard, or the ship could hit an uncharted reef and everyone could be drowned. Knowing your ropes is crucial. Not knowing them can kill you! When the *Endeavour* reaches Funchal, the capital of Madeira, the quartermaster, Alexander Weir, gets tangled up in the anchor's guide rope. He is dragged to the bottom of the sea and drowned.

SUICIDE. Marine Private William Greenslade commits suicide by jumping overboard after being accused of theft.

TOO MUCH RUM. John Reading, age 24, dies from alcohol poisoning.

DROWNED. Peter Flowers, age 18, drowns at Rio de Janeiro. He has served with Captain Cook for five years.

Rations: food and drink

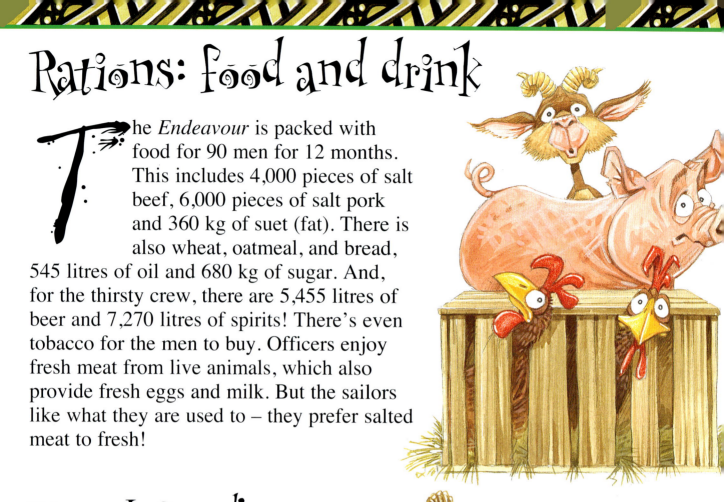

The *Endeavour* is packed with food for 90 men for 12 months. This includes 4,000 pieces of salt beef, 6,000 pieces of salt pork and 360 kg of suet (fat). There is also wheat, oatmeal, and bread, 545 litres of oil and 680 kg of sugar. And, for the thirsty crew, there are 5,455 litres of beer and 7,270 litres of spirits! There's even tobacco for the men to buy. Officers enjoy fresh meat from live animals, which also provide fresh eggs and milk. But the sailors like what they are used to – they prefer salted meat to fresh!

Dinner Is Served!

Not more fresh meat!

I need the limes to help my teeth stay healthy!

Handy hint

It's best to eat the ship's biscuits in the dark, so you can't see the pesky weevils!

SAUERKRAUT. This pickled cabbage contains vitamins that help prevent a disease called scurvy, which makes your teeth fall out. There are 3,565 kg of it on board. But the men will only eat it after they see the officers eating it. Limes and syrup of lemons can also help to prevent outbreaks of scurvy.

23

Landfall!

A fter stopping at the Atlantic island of Madeira, you cross the Equator, and pick up supplies at Rio de Janeiro, in Brazil. Finally you reach Cape Horn. Joseph Banks and his team collect specimens at Tierra del Fuego, and Cook makes surveys of sheltered places to anchor. Soon, you are clear of stormy Cape Horn. The *Endeavour* sails northwest to the newly discovered island of Tahiti in the Pacific. You reach it on 13th April, 1769 – in time to observe the transit of Venus in June.

JOSEPH BANKS. He collects specimens from wherever he can and takes them back to the ship to study.

TIERRA DEL FUEGO. The people here live in huts of woven tree-trunks. Captain Cook writes, "They are neither proof against wind, hail, rain or snow … these people must be a hardy race."

24

Handy hint

Never look at the sun through a telescope. You will burn your eyes and go BLIND!!

I hope the sky's not cloudy!

THE PEOPLE OF TAHITI. These friendly people don't understand private property. They'll take anything that's left lying around! (below)

COOK'S OBSERVATIONS
Captain Cook recorded his observations of the transit (as shown right).

25

Tattoos and canoes

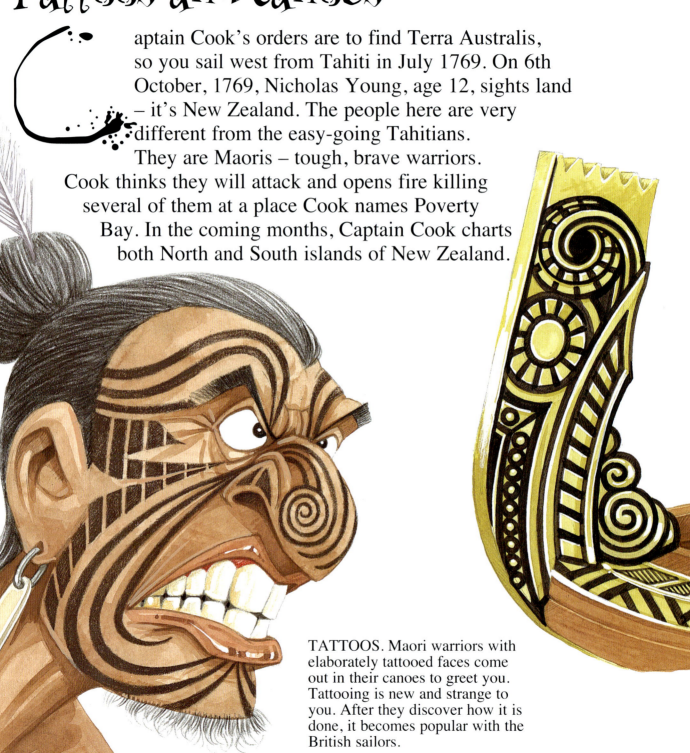

Captain Cook's orders are to find Terra Australis, so you sail west from Tahiti in July 1769. On 6th October, 1769, Nicholas Young, age 12, sights land – it's New Zealand. The people here are very different from the easy-going Tahitians. They are Maoris – tough, brave warriors. Cook thinks they will attack and opens fire killing several of them at a place Cook names Poverty Bay. In the coming months, Captain Cook charts both North and South islands of New Zealand.

TATTOOS. Maori warriors with elaborately tattooed faces come out in their canoes to greet you. Tattooing is new and strange to you. After they discover how it is done, it becomes popular with the British sailors.

Great Barrier of grief!

After charting New Zealand, you sail northwest to find Terra Australis. On 18th January, Lieutenant Hicks sights land. On 29th April, you anchor at a sheltered bay. Joseph Banks and his team collect a great number of new plants. There are so many that Cook names the place Botany Bay. Then you sail north again. Captain Cook is the first to chart the entire east coast of Australia.

NO THANKS. The Australian aborigines are not interested in trading or gifts.

CRASH! At the Great Barrier Reef, the ship strikes coral! A bandage made from a sail filled with wool and oakum is dragged over the hole. Water pressure keeps it in place.

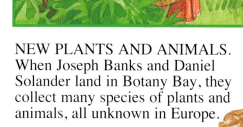

NEW PLANTS AND ANIMALS. When Joseph Banks and Daniel Solander land in Botany Bay, they collect many species of plants and animals, all unknown in Europe.

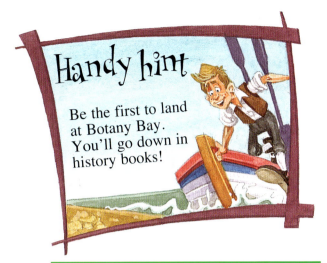

Handy hint

Be the first to land at Botany Bay. You'll go down in history books!

SOUNDINGS. The crew take soundings to get the ship through the reefs. On the shore, they spend seven weeks on repairs.

SAVE WEIGHT. To help refloat the ship, anchors, guns, cannon balls, iron pots and spare timbers are thrown overboard.

STUCK ON THE REEF. You and the crew work the pumps and plug the hole. After 24 hours, you manage to refloat the ship. You use longboats to tow it off the reef.

Come on! We've been stuck on this reef for 12 hours!

Disease, done for, and death!

eaving Australia, Cook anchors at the island of Savu for fresh supplies. The crew are in good health. Then you sail to Batavia (now called Jakarta), a Dutch settlement. You dock there in October 1770. Soon, men start to get sick with malaria. The disease takes hold. The first to die is the surgeon, William Monkhouse, on 5th November. Tents are set up ashore, where the sick can be better looked after. As you start for Cape Town, South Africa, 40 men are on the sick list. In 1771, between January and February, many of your shipmates die. Eleven are buried at sea in one week! In all, one-third of the crew die of malaria and dysentery, which is also called the 'bloody flux'.

BURIAL AT SEA. When a sailor dies, the sail-maker sews him into his hammock. A stitch is put through his nose to make sure he is dead. Cannon shot inside the canvas makes sure the body sinks.

WILLIAM MONKHOUSE. William Monkhouse is the surgeon until he dies. If a sick bay is needed at sea, a small area is canvassed off.

We need a bigger sick bay!

Land ahoy!

On 13th July, 1771, Nicholas Young sights Land's End, in Cornwall. You and your shipmates are excited to see the coast of England after three years at sea. The voyage has been a great success, apart from the crew losses. Cook has fulfilled the Admiralty's and the Royal Society's orders. The transit of Venus has been observed. The entire coastline of New Zealand is charted, and the coast of eastern Australia is mapped too.

MADEIRA

Atlantic Ocean

RIO DE JANEIRO

CAPE TOW

TIERRA DEL FUEG

THE ROUTE. This map shows the *Endeavour*'s route on the voyage between 1768 and 1771. This will become the blueprint for Captain Cook's future voyages in the South Seas.

Land ahoy!

Is it home, Captain?

Looks like Cornwall.

Pacific Ocean

BATAVIA (JAKARTA)

Indian Ocean

BOTANY BAY

TAHITI

Handy hint

Bring something from your travels as a gift for your parents!

HOME AGAIN! Your parents hardly recognize you. You join Captain Cook as master mate on his second voyage, on the *Resolution*. In 1787, you become a captain. In 1807, you're made a rear admiral!

NEW LAND TO RULE. The government can now see new places for Britain to rule. Captain Cook is soon sent on a second expedition in two larger ships: *Resolution* and *Adventure*, 1772–1775.

Welcome home my boy! What have you brought me?

Glossary

Admiralty The government department responsible for the British Royal Navy.

Astronomer A scientist who studies the stars and other heavenly bodies.

Boatswain/Bosun The officer in charge of the sails and rigging. His duties include waking up the men for their duty.

Botanists Scientists who study plant life.

Brimstone The old word for sulphur.

Chart To make a map of coastlines in detail so ships can navigate. It can also mean the map itself.

Cutlass A short sword with a slightly curved blade used by sailors.

Dysentery An infectious disease that causes very bad diarrhoea.

Equator An imaginary line making a circle around Earth, halfway between the North and South Poles.

Fumigate To use smoke to kill germs.

Grog A seaman's daily allowance of rum.

Malaria A fever caused by a tiny parasite, carried and spread by mosquitoes.

Oakum Loose fibres made by picking old rope into pieces.

Ratline A short rope fastened across two shrouds to form a ladder on a boat.

Rigging The ropes, sails and stays of a ship.

Scurvy A serious disease that many sailors used to suffer from, caused by a lack of Vitamin C. This was because of the shortage of fresh fruit and vegetables in their diet.

Shrouds A set of ropes forming the rigging for the masts.

Square-rigger A sailing ship with the sail rig set at right angles to the mast and keel.

Transit The route of a star or planet as seen from Earth.

Index

Scientific sensation

The fact that Joseph Banks' inclusion on the voyage was such a success meant that it became common for scientists to accompany naval voyages of exploration. The samples of animal and plant life brought back from these expeditions captured the public's imagination and stimulated desire for knowledge about far-flung parts of the world.

In the long-term, with the discoveries made by such figures as Charles Darwin when he sailed with the *Beagle* in the early 19th century, these treasures from the New World would soon start to reshape people's understanding of natural and human history.

The controversy surrounding these developments gave rise to religious and philosophical debates that are still raging to this day.

The history of exploration

European countries have always had a thirst for exploration. Many places in America and Australia were discovered by the Dutch and the Portuguese. The British Empire had a massive Royal Navy that it used to explore far-off lands and chart them on maps. This helped our understanding of the world around us. Captain Cook was one, very important, part of this process that started long before him and continues to this day. There is always something new to learn about our world.

The Age of Discovery lasted from the end of the 15th century to the 18th. This was a time when the whole of Europe was setting sail and trying to find as many new places as they could. Christopher Columbus is one of the most famous sailors and explorers ever. In 1492, he discovered America, leading to settlement there by people from across Europe.

In 1519, Ferdinand Magellan, a Portuguese explorer, set off on a voyage that would be the first one to travel all around the world. This is called circumnavigation and it was incredibly important for discovering new lands, new plants and new people.

After Captain Cook's adventures, many more discoveries were made. Navies went to the farthest reaches of the world, exploring places like Antarctica and the North Pole. Almost the entire world has been charted on maps now, and we think we have a pretty good idea of where everything is. But we still have that itch to explore and to discover new places.

Captain Cook's top contributions

Cartography (the science of drawing maps)

Cook created maps and charts that were more accurate than any that had come before. This was a very complicated process. He had to measure the angle between the moon and the sun (or the moon and a specific star if it was nighttime). This allowed him to work out the time back home in England. By comparing that to the time wherever he was, he was able to chart the longtitude of his location, and this made it possible to create really accurate maps. (This was much easier to do once he brought a clock along!)

Sailors' diets

Another astounding feat at the time was that Cook managed to sail all around the world (circumnavigate) without losing a single sailor to scurvy. This was a common disease for sea travellers and was caused by a lack of vitamins.

Cook made sure to always have fresh food supplies and medicine on board, which prevented the disease. This influenced the way sea travel was conducted from then on.

Plant life

Cook and his botanists (scientists who study plant life) discovered over 3,000 new species of plant. These were very valuable to British scientists back home.

World's first animal tourist

We can't ignore one of Cook's most important achievements. He owned the first animal to circumnavigate the globe – his pet goat!